Prehistoric Man

RUPERT OLIVER

Illustrated by

BERNARD LONG

GALLERY BOOKS
An Imprint of W. H. Smith Publishers Inc.
112 Madison Avenue
New York City 10016

First published in Great Britain in 1983 by
Hodder and Stoughton Children's Books

This edition published in 1990 by Gallery Books
An imprint of W.H. Smith Publishers Inc.
112 Madison Avenue
New York 10016

By arrangement with Octopus Books Limited

Copyright © 1983 Martspress Ltd.

ISBN 0-8317-7136-4

Printed in Portugal

Contents

The First Link

Today man has set foot on the moon and is surrounded by all the benefits of twentieth century civilisation. But there was a time, not very long ago in our world's history, when man dressed in skins and lived in caves. It has taken man just a few thousand years to change from caveman to spaceman. Though this period of time includes all the history which has ever been written, it seems very short indeed when compared to the many millions of years which it took man to evolve from his animal forebears.

The first link in the long chain of human evolution lived sixty million years ago in North America. Today scientists call it the *Plesiadapis gidleyi*.

When the *Plesiadapis* was alive the world was very different from the way it is today. The many species of animals would all have been very strange to our eyes and, of course, there were no men walking the earth. In fact it was only about six million years earlier that the mighty dinosaurs had died out.

When the dinosaurs disappeared they left open many ecological niches for the tiny mammals to exploit. A niche is a particular way of life which is suited to one animal. For instance the giraffe has filled a niche by evolving a long neck so that it can eat the leaves from the tops of trees. One of the niches left open was exploited by a group of mammals known as the primates. Today the primate group includes all the monkeys, apes and man.

The *Plesiadapis* belonged to a group of very primitive primates known as *prosimiae*. Though the *Plesiadapis* itself was probably too specialised to be an ances-

tor of man, it does give us a good idea of the appearance of man's early primate ancestors.

It is thought that this small tree-living primate was very good at leaping around in the trees looking for the juicy leaves and fruits on which it fed. Though the *Plesiadapis* spent a lot of time in the trees it almost certainly liked to visit the ground from time to time. It may have done this to collect fruit that had fallen from above or simply to cross from one tree to the next.

As time passed and the descendants of *Plesiadapis* and other similar primates evolved in such a way as to be suited to a life in the trees, the primate group divided into several families. It was at this stage that the ancestors of man split from the ancestors of the apes and the monkeys. Unfortunately there are very few primate fossils dating from this

The seventy-centimetres-long *Plesiadapis* lived about fifty-eight million years ago in North America. It was one of the earliest primates.

period so scientists do not know exactly what these early hominids were like. Hominids is the name given to man and his ancestors. This separates them from pongids, apes and their ancestors.

However, we do know that twenty-eight million years ago in what is now Egypt there lived a primate known as the *Aegyptopithecus zeuxis*. As can be seen in our picture of this creature, the *Aegyptopithecus* is far more advanced than the *Plesiadapis* and is clearly recognisable as a primate.

This creature had a strange mixture of advanced and primitive characteristics. We know that it was probably an ancestor of the apes because it had some very specialised teeth, typical of the pongids. However, despite being an ape, the

9

Aegyptopithecus had a tail, which is a feature not usually found in pongids. This, together with the rather small braincase, was probably an evolutionary leftover from its more primitive ancestors. It was soon lost in the course of evolution.

On the other hand, the *Aegyptophithe-cus* had perfect binocular vision, an advanced feature found in later pongids. Binocular vision means that both eyes face forwards. This adaptation made the *Aegyptopithecus* expert at judging distances. So it was able to leap around the trees far more safely and with greater speed than many earlier primates.

The fossils of *Aegyptopithecus zeuxis*, which represents an important stage in the evolution of the primates, have been found in Egypt.

The halfway stage of the *Aegyptopithecus* gives us a good idea of the probable appearance of man's ancestors when they reached a similar stage of evolution.

The Seed-eaters

Over the page can be seen a hominid which is very important to scientists. It is known as the *Ramapithecus punjabicus* and may be the oldest known ancestor of man.

The *Ramapithecus* lived in the foothills of the Himalayas, in India, about ten million years ago. It is thought that it ate seeds, roots and the odd small animal which were plentiful in the area. The *Ramapithecus* was probably able to stand upright on two legs, but there is not enough fossil evidence for the scientists to be sure whether or not it could walk on two legs.

Recent study of the *Ramapithecus* fossils has given rise to a new theory on the evolution of man. It was previously believed that man was forced to make weapons and to evolve a more intelligent brain because his body was so weak when compared to wild animals. Then because primitive men developed better minds and tools they did not need such powerful bodies. This meant that the evolution of man tended towards a more intelligent brain and a weaker body.

This theory works well, but there is a problem. It assumes that the ancestors of man were already living on the plains, had evolved hands and were rather more intelligent than other animals. It was to cover this gap that the new seed-eater theory was devised.

The *Aegyptopithecus* probably lived similarly to some of today's monkeys, climbing the trees, eating fruit, leaves and the occasional small animal. However the *Aegyptopithecus* was certainly an ape, and was evolving in a different way from the ancestors of the monkeys, which lived at the same time.

11

This theory argued that a primitive hominid left the forest and took to a life on the plains eating seeds and roots. When eating, the creature would have sat upright, using its hands to pick up food. If this picture is correct it would explain much about the early evolution of the hominids. Because the body was held upright the spine would have evolved in such a way that upright walking was possible. As the creature had to pick up small objects, such as grass seeds, it would have needed to evolve hands capable of gripping and holding a variety of objects.

The creature would now have the capability to begin the evolution towards man according to the traditional theory.

The *Ramapithecus* appears to have evolved to the seed-eater stage. The teeth of the *Ramapithecus* were broad and flat, an adaptation to eating tough foods, such as seeds. We have very few fossils of the *Ramapithecus*, but it would appear to have been about one metre tall. It may have had a brain capacity of around three hundred and fifty cubic centimetres. This would have been small compared to that of modern man and no different from that of small apes, such as the chimpanzee.

The fossils of the *Ramapithecus* have not only been found in Northern India. Teeth and parts of skulls from *Ramapithecus* have been found in China and fossils have also turned up in Africa. This in itself is important for it shows that man's possible ancestors may have been widely distributed from the earliest stages of hominid evolution.

This poses another problem for scien-

The *Ramapithecus* represents the 'seed-eater' stage of human evolution, but it is not certain that man is descended from this creature.

tists. Did these early hominids evolve towards man all over the Earth at the same time, or did one group of hominids evolve and then spread out over the world later?

At present we do not know the answer to this question. As with many of the unsolved problems about man's evolution we must wait for the scientists to discover more fossils and to carry out more research.

Upright Apes in Africa

As the years went by the evolution of the hominids continued and by three million years ago the group known as *Australopithecine* was walking the earth. The group is divided into two genera. First there is a smaller, more man-like creature called the *Australopithecus africanus* and secondly a larger creature known as the *Paranthropus*.

The *Paranthropus* was larger than any previous hominid, standing about one and a half metres tall, and very heavily built with thick bones and large muscles. The various species of *Paranthropus* were probably highly developed seed-eater hominids which never progressed along the road to man but became a dead end in man's evolutionary path.

It is thought that the *Paranthropus* lived in open woodland or at the edges of forests, where there would have been a good supply of plant food. Although it could walk upright on two legs the *Paranthropus* was perhaps not very adept at it. The big toe is thought to have been set at an awkward angle so the creature would have walked with a stoop and a pronounced roll.

The skull of the *Paranthropus* was well adapted to a life of eating coarse plant food. Along the top of the skull was a bony ridge running from front to back; to this ridge were attached very powerful jaw muscles. These muscles, together with the strong, flat teeth, were used to grind down seeds and other plant material. The success of the *Paranthropus* is shown by the fact that it survived for around three million years, only becoming extinct about one million years ago.

It should be pointed out that some scientists think that the *Paranthropus* was part of the *Australopithecus* genus and not an independent line.

The *Australopithecus africanus* was not only shorter than the *Paranthropus*, but it also lacked the thick bones and general robustness of its larger contemporary. The *Australopithecus* stood about one and a quarter metres tall; it could walk and run on two legs much better than the *Paranthropus*, though it also did so with a slight roll.

The *Australopithecus* had evolved well past the seed-eater stage of the *Ramapithecus* and represents a crucial phase in the evolution of the hominids. It was probably the earliest creature which walked upright and used tools to obtain food.

The *Australopithecus* probably lived on open grassland or in some of the forests where there was plenty of room to move around. Not only did it eat fruit and roots but it ate meat as well. This new trait in diet may have been due to a change in climate

When the *Ramapithecus* lived millions of years earlier there was enough plant food available all year round, but if the climate had altered so that there was not enough plant food during the winter the

The evolutionary line which led to the *Paranthropus* was a dead end. The creatures became extinct about one million years ago.

descendants of *Ramapithecus* would
have had to take to eating meat during
that part of the year.

At first the upright apes would have
scavenged meat from the kills of lions
and other predators. This could have
been achieved quite easily by a group of
about ten hominids if they worked
together. Having found a lion with a
fresh kill they could have advanced
shouting and waving sticks. Such a dis-
play would have frightened a single lion
away.

Soon after the *Australopithecus* hunted
in Africa, there lived a hominid about
which there has been much argument.
Scientists cannot even agree about its
name.

16

This hominid was rather more advanced than the average *Australopithecus*. Because of these differences some scientists think that it was a primitive man and have called it *Homo habilis*, which means 'handy man'. But other scientists think that it was only an advanced species of *Australopithecus* and have named it *Australopithecus*

Homo habilis, thought by many scientists to be the first man, was probably able to organise hunting parties.

habilis, the handy southern ape.

The question of whether to call this creature *Homo* or *Australopithecus* is very important, for to name it *Homo* would be to accept it as a member of the same

17

genus as modern man, rather than to treat it as an ape which is almost a man. The main problem is that scientists are not quite sure where to place the border-line between a primitive man and an advanced hominid ape.

What kind of creature was *habilis* and why is there so much confusion? *Habilis* looked very much like an *Australopithecus* though he was slightly taller, standing about one and a third metres tall. He was also able to walk much better, almost as well as modern man. But despite these differences *habilis* was still very much like an *Australopithecus* as far as his skeleton is concerned. It is because of these similarities that many scientists say that *habilis* was a type of *Australopithecus* and not a man, or *Homo*.

However, other scientists maintain that a fossil hominid should be called a man if it is capable of intelligent thought. By this definition they argue that *habilis* was a man because of some remarkable finds.

In the same area and dating from the same time as *habilis* have been found a large number of stone tools, some of which can be seen below. It is true that these tools are rather simple and primitive but even so whoever made them must have been intelligent enough to realise how useful they were and how to make them. This represents a dramatic step in the evolution of man. For the first time the ancestors of man could change the environment to suit themselves rather than just try to survive in a hostile world.

The tools themselves fall into two distinct types of toolmaking, known as cultures. The earlier is called the Oldowan culture and it produced one basic tool. This tool was made by chipping flakes off a large pebble, leaving a sharp edge on the pebble which was useful for chopping up meat. For this reason the tool is known as a chopper.

The later culture, known as Acheulean, was more advanced than the Oldowan culture. There were at least twelve types of Acheulean tool including axes, picks, chisels, scrapers and hammers.

Because of the variety and skill of the tools it is clear that *habilis* was more intelligent than previous hominids. But the problem of whether this makes *habilis* a man or not will probably not be solved until more fossils are found and scientists have had a chance to do more research on this remarkable creature.

Left, the controversial *Homo habilis* lived in Africa about two million years ago.
Below, some of the tools associated with *Homo habilis* and with his successor *Homo erectus*.

The First Men

Though scientists may argue about whether or not *habilis* was a man and whether he was an ancestor of present-day man or not, no one doubts that *Homo erectus* was a man. The name means upright man and it is clear from fossils and other finds that *Homo erectus* was a man with a complex way of life.

We know that *Homo erectus* was about one and a half metres tall, rather shorter than modern man. He had a stocky, muscular build, well suited to a hard life spent hunting animals and gathering wild plants. The bones of *Homo erectus* that have been found by scientists show us that this prehistoric man had very strong limbs, the bones being both thicker and heavier than those of modern man. However despite these differences the body of the *Homo erectus*

was much the same as that of modern man. The evolution of man since the time of *Homo erectus* has been mainly concerned with the brain and head.

The forehead of the *Homo erectus* sloped backwards dramatically, limiting the brain volume to around one thousand cubic centimetres. Modern man has a brain volume of about one thousand four hundred cubic centimetres. Above the eyes ran a very pronounced bony ridge which, together with a receding chin, gave *Homo erectus* a distinctive profile.

By the time of *Homo erectus* a feature that is unique to man had evolved. He had lost his hairy coat. Scientists are not quite sure why man lost his covering of fur, but perhaps the reason lies in the way of life of early man.

These men lived an active life running around on the hot plains of Africa and Asia, hunting and gathering food. Other animals that live in the same way, such as lions and cheetahs, lose heat by panting.

But primates, including man, cannot pant. The only way the early men could have kept cool was to sweat. A thick coat of hair would obviously hamper the cooling process. Over countless generations of evolution man's ancestors lost their insulating hair and gained thousands upon thousands of sweat glands all over the body, so solving the problem of keeping cool.

This adaptation to the heat of the tropics had an unfortunate side effect. It meant that early hominids were unprotected against the colder climates of Europe and northern Asia. As a result vast areas of the world were closed to man, until *Homo erectus* made one of the most important discoveries of prehistory.

He discovered fire.

Fires and Huts

As with so many things concerned with the prehistory of man we do not know just how fire was first discovered, nor how it was tamed.

When the first men encountered fire in nature, perhaps as a forest fire, there can be no doubt that they were terrified. The awesome destructiveness of fire has made virtually every animal recognise it as a deadly enemy.

As man's intelligence increased, his terror must have turned to curiosity. He would have realised that fire gave out heat and during a long, cold winter heat was essential to survival. Perhaps one *Homo erectus*, more adventurous than the rest, picked up a burning branch from a forest fire and took it back to camp. Once the fire had been captured it had to be kept alight by feeding it with more dry branches.

Fire did not only keep a group of *Homo erectus* warm during the winter but it cooked food for them as well. If some careless *Homo erectus* dropped a piece of meat into the fire he would probably have been upset at losing some food. But if he was able to retrieve the piece of meat later, when the fire had died down, he would have found that it tasted nicer and was not so tough to chew. Soon *Homo erectus* learnt to cook his food instead of eating it raw.

But the discovery and mastery of fire had far wider implications than keeping man warm in winter and cooking his food.

The warmth of fire meant that man could explore vast new areas of land as he pushed north into the colder climates

Man first appeared about one million years ago in the shape of *Homo erectus*. By five hundred thousand years ago he had learnt to use fire.

20

Homo erectus was a skilled hunter. Using fire-hardened spears, he was able to track down and kill many types of animal, though vegetable food may have been the mainstay of his diet.

previously denied to him. So the influence of man on his environment was not only increasing at this time but it was spreading over the globe as well.

Because of its very nature a fire has to have a hearth and has to remain in one position. This meant that for the first time man had a centre to group around and relax. One *Homo erectus* hearth in China has been found to have a pile of ashes seven metres deep, so the band must have stayed in one place for some generations.

As the groups of *Homo erectus* sat around the hearth well into the evening, one can conjecture that they may have communicated verbally to each other, in which case they probably discussed their everyday pursuits.

Whether they argued about the hunt, the weather or anything else, these discussions were important towards the development of language into a far more subtle method of communication than it had ever been before.

We have seen that fire was important, for it gave man heat and a social centre which were both vital to the future cultural development of man from the simple hunter-gatherer to the civilisation of the present day.

The use of fire was not the only great step forward that *Homo erectus*, the first definite man, took towards civilisation. He also began to build huts in which to live.

In the south of France, near the modern holiday town of Nice, scientists have found the remains of some huts which are probably some four hundred thousand years old. From the remains it is possible to reconstruct the hut shown overleaf and how its builders lived.

The hut was built of saplings, braced around the base with stones. Though this may have provided shelter from the sun and the rain, it would have been very draughty. For this reason the hearth in the hut was surrounded by a windbreak of stones. Different areas within the hut and around it were used for varying purposes.

In one place the toolmaker of the group chipped away at stones and bones to make many types of tools. He left behind him a large amount of stone chippings which have given modern scientists valuable information about how tools were made nearly half a million years ago. In another area, close to the hearth, was a large flat stone on which meat was chopped up.

The hut was used as a seasonal home for the band of hunters which built it. Scientists have been able to prove this because vast numbers of bones from young deer and ibex have been found. These young animals are born in the spring so the hut must have been inhabited during the early summer. The band would have left for another home during the autumn and winter because the hut was abandoned and rebuilt at the same season each year. In fact the hut was rebuilt at least eleven times.

It can be seen that *Homo erectus* was a true man, not only in evolutionary terms but also culturally. The stage was set for the emergence of our own species, *Homo sapiens*, some two hundred and fifty thousand years ago.

Intelligent Man arrives

Modern man is a member of the species *Homo sapiens*. This species is itself divided into several subspecies, one of the oldest of which lived a quarter of a million years ago in Western Europe. It is known today as *Homo sapiens steinheimensis* because a fossil of this man was first found near the town of Steinheim in Germany.

The evolution of man from *Homo erectus* to *Homo sapiens* can be traced in the fossils which these men have left behind. *Homo sapiens* fossils have a much larger brain and a smaller, less rugged face than those of *Homo erectus*.

Though early subspecies of *Homo sapiens*, such as *Homo sapiens steinheimensis*, are classed in the same species as modern man, there were still major differences between them and us.

Overleaf can be seen a *Homo erectus* encampment near the Mediterranean. This site has been excavated by scientists in recent years.

Steinheim man had very heavy ridges of bone above his eyes. These brow ridges hardly exist at all in modern man. A heavy jaw and receding chin were also prominent in the face of this early man and were both primitive features soon to be lost in the course of evolution.

As time passed, man continued to evolve and by about one hundred and fifty thousand years ago perhaps the best-known prehistoric man had appeared, Neanderthal man.

Neanderthal man, or *Homo sapiens neanderthalensis* (named after the Neanderthal valley in Germany where the first skull of this species was discovered), was the last of the extinct men and was much more like modern man than even Steinheim man. He could walk and run like modern man and his brain size was large enough to be placed well within the variations of modern man. But he was a distinct subspecies nonetheless.

On the whole Neanderthal man was rather short, having an average height of about one and two-thirds metres. His body and limbs were stockier and stronger than those of modern man. He also retained the receding chin and sloping forehead of earlier, more primitive men.

However, these differences from modern man were not as great as has been supposed. A Neanderthal would be instantly recognisable as a human being and would have possessed considerable intelligence. He was by no means the shambling brute so often portrayed. It has been suggested that Neanderthal man's stocky build was a direct adaptation to the harsh climate in which he was forced to live, for many Neanderthals lived during the last Ice Age which began seventy thousand years ago.

A Time of Ice and Snow

The Ice Ages are amongst the strangest phenomena in the history of the Earth. During the past three million years mighty glaciers hundreds of kilometres long have advanced and retreated at least eight times.

As the great rivers of ice swept down from the mountains a number of dramatic changes came over the earth. Most noticeable of these changes was the change in climate, for the weather of the whole world became colder. In Northern Europe this meant that vast stretches of land were buried under tons of ice, some of the glaciers being three thousand metres thick. At one time the whole of Britain north of the Thames was covered by ice.

Further south, land not actually covered by the ice was seriously affected by it. Much of what is now fertile land was then tundra. Tundra is the name given to the type of vegetation which grows in very cold lands, where there are no trees and the country suffers long, harsh winters.

During the most recent Ice Age life became harder and harder, so many animals evolved so as to stand a better chance of survival in the cold weather. The woolly mammoth and the woolly rhinoceros are perhaps the most famous of these. It was in such an inhospitable world as this that Neanderthal man had to survive.

Faced with this challenge the Neanderthals of Europe had to use every means at their disposal to combat the cold and to find enough food. Fire had been inherited from their *Homo erectus*

Bands of *Homo erectus* were often in danger because of attacks of carnivores of the time.

forebears and was of immense importance during the long cold years of the Ice Age. It is also probable that Neanderthal man, living in a cool climate, wore some sort of clothing, more than likely of animal skins. Regrettably, to date, no trace has been found of any such clothing. Certain artefacts, though, *have* been discovered – scrapers, for example, which it is feasible to believe were used for cleaning skins before they were cured over a fire. Borers have also been unearthed and it is surmised that these were employed in boring holes in garments which were sewn together with strips of rawhide.

All these indications point strongly to a widespread use of furs as clothes.

During the past three million years several periods of cold climate, the Ice Ages, have brought arctic weather to Europe.

The stone tools of Neanderthal man were far more advanced than earlier examples. They are known as Mousterian tools, named after the town of Le Moustier in France, where they were first found.

For hundreds of thousands of years, ever since the time of *habilis*, man had been producing tools by the core technique. Using this method a man would select a stone of roughly the right size and shape and then chip away at it until a sharp edge was produced, as shown in the frontispiece. Hand-axes, usually produced by this method, have been found at many prehistoric sites.

Not only was this method of producing tools slow and time-consuming, but also the number of different tools which could be produced was very limited.

When a prehistoric man was making a

hand-axe using the core technique he would have c'_pped a lot of flakes away from the central stone. At first he may have ignored them as rubbish; but as the generations passed, toolmakers began to take more of an interest in these flakes.

The flakes were much sharper than the core tool, but being thinner they tended to break more easily. Nonetheless prehistoric toolmakers began to use the flakes for jobs, such as cutting up meat, where a sharp edge was needed.

The Mousterian culture of stone tools was based on the use of the flakes instead of the core. Instead of obtaining flakes merely as a by-product of making a core tool, Mousterian toolmakers struck the core so as deliberately to produce flakes. Eventually so many flakes would have been struck that the core became very small and had to be thrown away because it was useless.

Neanderthal man was very skilled at producing flake tools. He found that he could produce different tools not only by hitting the core in a different place but also by hitting it at a different angle or with more force. The size and shape of the flake could even be controlled by the Neanderthal by hitting the core with an antler instead of another stone. The softer antler produced a different shape of flake from that produced by a stone.

It is interesting to note that not all Mousterian tools are the same. They varied slightly from place to place. In one area there were far more scrapers than elsewhere, whilst in another place nearly all the tools had serrated edges, like a saw. We do not know why, but perhaps it was because Neanderthal

man needed different tools to survive in different environments. For instance serrated tools may have been of more use in a forest than out on the tundra.

Armed with these new weapons of stone, Neanderthal man was a far more successful hunter than his ancestors had been. The bones of reindeer, ibex, elk, and even elephants have been found at Neanderthal sites.

In order to hunt these large creatures the Neanderthals not only needed better weapons but also more successful hunting techniques. In order to catch the largest and most dangerous of animals, such as elephants, the wily hunters may have dug pits underneath forest tracks into which the beasts could fall.

Another successful method was to drive animals over cliffs or sudden drops. At the foot of one cliff in southern France the bones of thousands of horses have been found piled metres deep. Presumably the cliff was used many times to drive small herds over the edge until there were thousands of horse skeletons there. This probably took hundreds of years.

It has been estimated that the average band of twenty Neanderthals needed about five hundred pounds of meat each week in order to survive. Despite the resourcefulness of the hunters and their new weapons they could not always provide this amount of food.

A large proportion of the meat consumed by Neanderthals was from small animals such as rabbits and hares. It is thought that whilst the full-grown men were out hunting the big game the young boys may have spent their time hunting smaller creatures. The boys

Through time the style of tools and the way they were made has changed. Neanderthal and later people modified flakes struck from a core.

31

Children may sometimes have helped to catch small animals which were an important source of food.

would hunt with small spears or by throwing small sticks weighted at one end with stones. No doubt the youngsters found this great fun, but it was also very important for them and for their band.

As well as providing a welcome addition to the food supply the boys were learning the basic skills of hunting. They learnt how to track animals without being seen themselves. The constant practice of throwing weapons at fast-moving quarry was invaluable in their later life, for without it they could not have survived.

The life of a typical band of Neanderthals would have been a roaming, nomadic one. Their hunter-gatherer way of life depended on being able to cover a large area of land to find fresh hunting grounds. Or they may have followed the large herds of animals as they migrated south in the winter and north again for the summer.

The Original Caveman

During the winter the Neanderthals of Europe would have had to protect themselves from the bitter Ice Age weather. There is much evidence to suggest that they spent the winter sheltering in caves, and it was this habit which earned early man the collective name of cavemen.

Though caves gave protection against the winter gales and storms they could still be cold and draughty places. To

remedy this the Neanderthals kept fires burning within the cave to heat it up and they probably stretched a curtain of skins across the entrance in an effort to keep out draughts.

But Neanderthal man did not use caves only to live in. Some caves were used for a quite different and very mysterious reason.

Scientists investigating a cave high up in the Alps made a very strange discovery one day. Deep in the heart of the cave they found a large chest made of stones and inside were the skulls of seven cave bears. All of the skulls had been placed so that they were facing towards the entrance of the cave. Further in the cave another six bear skulls were found resting on ledges set high up on the walls.

These skulls were obviously placed there very deliberately by the Neanderthals, but why? The most likely explanation is that they were connected with some kind of hunting magic. It could be that Neanderthals believed that killing a bear at the beginning of the year would ensure good hunting for the rest of the season. Or maybe they thought that by eating the flesh of the bear they would gain some of its strength and knowledge of other animals. Whatever reason Neanderthal man had for hunting the cave bear, the hunt itself was far from easy.

The cave bear, known scientifically as *Ursus spelaeus*, was much larger than any bear alive today. When it reared up on its hind legs it would have stood a good metre taller than any of its hunters. Such a powerful and dangerous quarry must have been very difficult to kill and no

33

doubt many Neanderthals died in the attempt. It is thought that the bears were hunted during the winter when they were drowsy because of hibernation and not as dangerous as at other times of the year.

The existence of such a cult puts Neanderthal man well above the level of the animals for it shows he was concerned for the future and was capable of abstract thought.

A ritual which is perhaps more touching and closer to our own world is the fact that the Neanderthals buried their dead. Scientists have found the remains of many of these burials. In some cases the dead man or woman was buried with numerous stone tools, presumably owned by him or her during life. One of the graves contained the remains of dozens of flowers. It would appear that Neanderthal society treated the dead with as much respect as present-day society does.

New People and New Weapons

The Neanderthals were a very successful people, but today another people inhabits the world, *Homo sapiens sapiens*, our own subspecies.

The spread of the new subspecies can be traced by studying the tools and skeletons which they left behind them. It appears from this evidence that *Homo sapiens sapiens* emerged about fifty thousand years ago in the Middle East and perhaps even earlier in Africa.

Some Neanderthals lived in the Middle East but did not have the extreme features of their European cousins. Their skulls were not as long. This led many scientists to think that these Neanderthals were the ancestors of modern man. However the skull of modern man is quite distinct from that of the Neanderthals. The face is more upright, the braincase more vaulted and the chin is very much in evidence. The skull of the men from the Middle East was, according to some experts, a stage midway between the two.

By about thirty thousand years ago the new type of man had completely replaced the Neanderthals. But no one is quite sure just how this happened. Some scientists think that modern man evolved in the Middle East and then rapidly spread out over the world, killing off the native Neanderthals as he went. It is thought that they were able to do this because of their superior intelligence and culture.

Scientists, who support this view, point to the many recent examples of a more advanced culture taking over a less advanced one. Perhaps the most significant of these is the spread of white people across the great plains of North America. The plains were originally inhabited by American Indians who lived by hunting the buffalo. But when the white man arrived in vastly superior numbers and with much better weapons, he was easily able to remove the Indians and live on the plains himself. It is argued that a similar process removed the Neanderthals from Europe.

However more recent finds have been revealed which suggest that the spread of *Homo sapiens sapiens* did not mean the extermination of the Neanderthals. These new discoveries have led scientists to believe that the two populations assimilated each other by intermarriage.

It is also possible that the emergence of modern man was not confined to the

Deep in the heart of a mountain three Neanderthal hunters place the skull of a cave bear in a stone chest.

34

Middle East. If this is the case the local Neanderthals of Europe and elsewhere evolved into the new form of man at about the same time. Unfortunately, scientists have not found many fossils from the time of this crucial change-over period.

All that can be said with any certainty is that during the course of a few thousand years Neanderthal man was replaced by fully modern man. But how and why remain complete mysteries.

The emergence of Cro-Magnon man was accompanied by a dramatic rise in the level of toolmaking. Like Mousterian toolmakers the new craftsmen made great use of the flake technique for working flint and similar stone. However the new people introduced a fresh variation to this method. They produced a large number of blades. Blades are flakes struck from the core in a very special way so as to give an even longer cutting edge.

The whole period of *Homo sapiens sapiens* is marked by a continual flow of new ideas and techniques in the working of stone. Over the years dozens of new tools were produced. This process culminated in the Magdalenian culture which flourished some fifteen thousand years ago.

The Magdalenian toolmaker could produce about twelve metres of cutting edge from each pound of flint. This compares well with the one and a third metres of Neanderthal man and the eighteen centimetres of *Homo erectus*.

The tool kit of Cro-Magnon man not only included a wider range of stone tools but also tools made out of different materials. It was found that bone and wood could also be very useful. The wickedly barbed spearheads used to catch fish were made from bone, as were the needles which enabled the Cro-Magnon to sew together better clothes than his ancestors.

It is interesting to note that it was not until the end of Cro-Magnon times that arrowheads were produced. From this evidence it would seem that the enormous advantage of the bow was unknown to earlier men. The bow is a very efficient method of projecting a deadly missile a much greater distance than can be achieved simply by throwing. This invention gave Cro-Magnon man a considerable advantage in the hunt.

The Golden Age

The age of the Cro-Magnons was the golden age for man the hunter. Large herds of big game roamed the land and with his new weapons man could take full advantage of the situation.

One important fact regarding Cro-Magnon man should be noted. Skeletal remains of various kinds of Cro-Magnon man have been found all over the world – in Russia, Hungary, North and East Africa, China and South East Asia, South Africa and, surprisingly, in America and Australia.

In those far-off times, vast ice sheets spread across continents. Mighty ice-caps locked up much of the world's water and as a result sea levels dropped by as much as 125 metres. Thus huge areas of dry land were added to the continents. Venturesome Cro-Magnon men probably reached America after crossing Siberia for they would have been able to walk across the dry land bridge of Beringia to Alaska. The land bridge, of course, no longer exists. It is today the floor of the Bering Sea.

How Cro-Magnon men reached Australia is more of a mystery. It is surmised that the people living in South

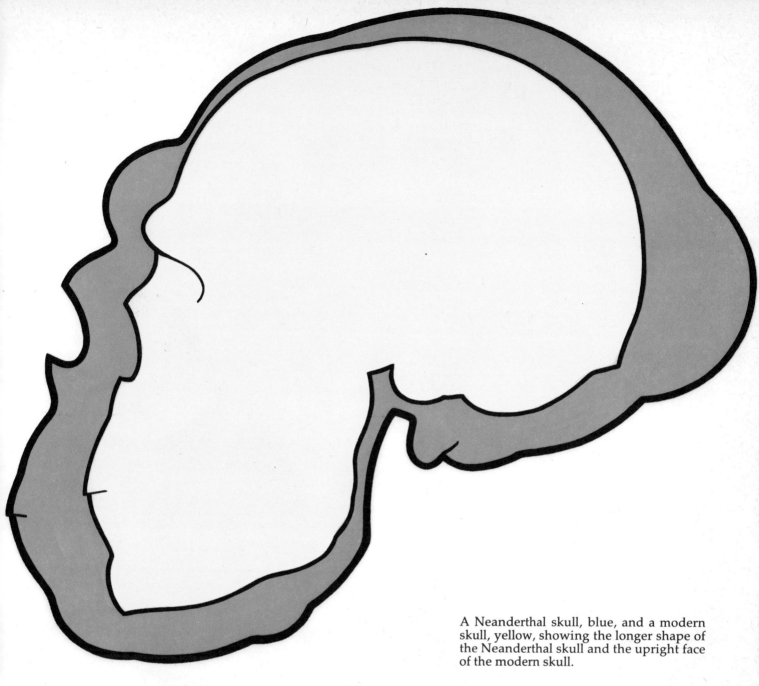

A Neanderthal skull, blue, and a modern skull, yellow, showing the longer shape of the Neanderthal skull and the upright face of the modern skull.

East Asia 30,000 years ago must have devised some form of sea craft. Assuming this, though, how did they happen to journey to Australia? Did the first arrivals know where they were going? If so, how? Were they carried there by some prevailing current? We do not know, but remains found there prove that Cro-Magnons *did* reach Australia.

In Europe at this time, some societies became almost dependent on hunting one particular animal. For example, the hunters living in present-day Ukraine hunted the woolly mammoth. A group of these hunters can be seen in the endpapers of this book.

The degree to which these ancient hunters depended on the mammoth can be deduced from their settlements. Even their huts were built from mammoth bones, as can be seen in the illustration, p.38. Because of the lack of trees out on the grassy steppes there was no wood with which to build huts. So the hunters used the long leg bones and tusks of their prey to build shelters. The homes of these Upper Palaeolithic hunters were often surprisingly large, some being as much as ten metres across.

A successful hunt must have been an event of great importance to a group of these people. Their whole way of life was based upon the mammoth. It was, of course, their main source of meat. Its

skin was used for clothing and for making the huts draught-proof. Its long shaggy hair could be used to make thread and the fat was probably used for lamps as well as food.

But of all the parts of a mammoth, perhaps the bones were the most useful.

While the longer bones were used to build huts, the short bones had their uses as well. If they were boiled to make soup they became an important source of food. They could also be ground down and used as fuel for the fires. A large number of these bones were, however, used to make delicate tools. Needles, fish-hooks, spear-throwers and barbed arrowheads were all made from bone.

The Upper Palaeolithic hunters of Eastern Europe thus depended on the mammoth for their survival.

It is probable that the hunters of this period, whether their quarry was mammoths, reindeer or smaller game, lived a kind of semi-nomadic life. Instead of wandering around haphazardly in pursuit of their game, they followed a set route throughout the year, having a permanent winter home and another for the summer.

But it should not be thought that hunting was the only source of food for Stone Age man. An important element of the diet was provided by the plants which grew all around. This source of food was very varied. Nuts, berries and roots were gathered when they were in season, together with the leaves of many plants.

Much of this food, particularly the nuts and roots, could be stored and

Left, a group of mammoth hunters, one of whom holds a bow which was first introduced about twelve thousand years ago, leaves their encampment in Eastern Europe. Overleaf, a favourite hunting trick was to drive the mammoth into marshy ground where it might become bogged down.

helped the band of hunter-gatherers to survive the winter when hunting was sparse.

In primitive societies, the often dangerous and arduous task of hunting has always been carried out by the men. This is not to say that the men would not have collected the vegetables; but it is likely that the women devoted a lot of their time to this task. In some areas, the collecting of plants was far more important to the survival of the band than the hunting of animals.

Just like their ancestors, early *Homo sapiens sapiens* lived by hunting and gathering, but there was one aspect of their life that marked them out from all previous men. They had invented art.

The Mysterious Caverns

The most famous examples of late Palaeolithic art are to be found deep under the ground. These are the great cave paintings. In hundreds of caverns, some set deep in the heart of the earth, early man created beautiful murals. Life-size horses and bison gallop across the walls and ceilings of these long-lost art galleries.

The paintings are all the more remarkable if we consider the simple materials available to the prehistoric artist. The paints were all made from natural pigments; for example, black was made from charcoal and red from ochre. These powders were then mixed with egg white, or sometimes blood, to make them into a liquid paint.

The paint was applied to the rock with equally simple tools – a sponge of moss, a plain hair brush or even just the artist's fingers. Yet with these simple methods prehistoric man created some staggeringly beautiful paintings. But why did he bother to paint at all?

The simplest explanation to our modern minds is that he enjoyed paintings and appreciated art. But the fact that so many of the paintings were executed hundreds of metres within caves where it was pitch black seems to rule out this possibility. In fact the curious positioning of the paintings may help to explain their purpose.

Because the paintings were set in caves difficult to reach it may be that they were placed there for some mystical reason. This suggestion is reinforced when it is remembered that they could only have been viewed by flickering torch and lantern light, which would cast strange and mysterious shadows around the cave.

For many years scientists have believed that the main reason for the cave paintings was 'hunting-magic'. It was noticed that most of the animals painted were those hunted by ancient man. It followed that the artist was trying to gain some control over his prey by painting its likeness on the wall. This was probably accompanied by a ritual of some kind.

For instance the newly painted animal may have been 'hunted' in a dance by a band of hunters, the ritual ending with the painting being pelted with spears, or a spear being added to the painting. In this way the men of twenty thousand years ago may have hoped to gain luck in the hunt. Some animals have indeed been found with arrows and spears painted on afterwards.

There can be little doubt that this accounts for some of the paintings, but why did prehistoric man paint so many

Using wicker baskets and leather bags, the Cro-Magnon women took care of the important job of collecting roots and berries.

bison when he spent so much of his time hunting reindeer?

There have been many theories put forward to explain this and other problems. It is possible that each band of hunters adopted a particular animal as a tribal emblem and painted it wherever they went. Or perhaps the caves were used to initiate boys into the privileged circle of full-grown hunters. But no one theory can account for all the paintings. It is probable that different artists painted for different reasons and enacted many strange and diverse rituals.

Though the cave paintings are the

44

most spectacular and famous examples of prehistoric art, they are not the only examples of primitive art. Hundreds of small stones have been found which have pictures of animals engraved on them.

It would seem that the people of the time were fond of jewellery in the form

It is thought that the beautifully painted Palaeolithic caves may have been used for strange ceremonies of some kind.

of bone and shell. These were made into bracelets, necklaces and other forms of adornment, some of them quite beautiful and delicate, requiring a high degree of skill to make them.

45

But the most mysterious artefacts from the Upper Palaeolithic period fall into none of these categories. The famous *batons de commandement* are too large to be considered as jewellery, but they also appear to be quite useless as weapons or anything else.

Though nobody is quite sure what these strange objects were for it is possible that the *batons de commandement* were symbolic objects. They were usually beautifully carved and were often buried with their owner. So it has been suggested that they were given to a man in recognition of some great deed or as a symbol of leadership.

The Mesolithic Era

During the most recent Ice Age man lived in a world ideally suited to his hunter-gatherer way of life. Vast herds of large animals roamed the plains and Cro-Magnon man, with his wide range of weapons, could take full advantage of this favourable situation.

But about sixteen thousand years ago the weather started to become warmer and the ice to retreat. Along with the climatic shift came a dramatic change in the environment. The great stretches of open tundra retreated, to be replaced by dense forest. As the tundra disappeared, so did the animals which had lived upon it. The reindeer could only survive in small numbers far to the north, while the woolly mammoth became totally extinct.

With his main source of food and clothing gone, man faced one of the greatest catastrophes in his entire history.

The disappearance of the great herds meant that man had to find new sources of food. In various parts of the world people found quite different ways to survive.

In North America the bison provided a good source of food until modern times. The situation in Europe and Asia was far more serious. In lands where the forests had taken over, man had to turn to hunting the new creatures of the woods. However these creatures, such as the red deer and wild boar, were far fewer in number than the Ice Age creatures had been. So these men could no longer live by relying on hunting. In an attempt to supplement their diet the bands took to eating much more plant food than before. The woodland offered a wider variety of berries and nuts than the Ice Age environment had done. It was this fundamental shift in diet that enabled man to survive in the heavily forested lands of Europe.

On the coasts around the continents and islands of the world people took to fishing. The settlements of these fishing folk can be quite clearly traced by today's scientists. At each settlement, the people left behind large mounds of rubbish, known as middens. These prehistoric rubbish tips reveal a lot about how the fishing men lived ten thousand years ago.

It is from studying the middens that scientists know of the many beautifully made tools and weapons of these people. But by far the most numerous finds in the middens are the remains of prehistoric man's meals. Thousands upon thousands of bones have been found by scientists. These show us that these ancient people not only caught fish but they also roamed the shoreline, picking up shellfish. In some areas they even took to the sea in dugout canoes in order to hunt seals.

After the disappearence of the great herds, people living near the coast took to a life of fishing and hunting seals.

This period of time, after the most recent Ice Age, when man was finding new ways to survive, is known as the Middle Stone Age or the Mesolithic Era.

The First Farmers

During the Mesolithic Era, there were people living in the Middle East who found an even better way to survive than anyone else.

They noticed that in the hills near where they lived there grew a very strange plant. It was a kind of grass, but it was larger than other grasses and had large seeds as well. These people, known to us as Natufians, soon found that the seeds of this plant were very good to eat, especially if they were first ground between two stones. The plants that the Natufians had discovered were the wild ancestors of wheat and barley.

For many years the Natufians lived by gathering the seeds of these plants each autumn and storing them to eat through the rest of the year. They also hunted the wild animals of the area.

Then about ten thousand years ago some of the Natufians began to plant their extra grain near their homes. This meant that in the autumn there would be plenty of food nearby instead of up in the hills.

The idea soon caught on and many villages in the Near East were surrounded by fields of golden wheat and barley. For the first time ever, man had a steady supply of food from one year to the next.

These people also began to herd together the wild sheep and goats which lived near their homes. The sheep and goats provided man with meat and also with clothes, for man soon learned to spin and to weave. The first agriculture had been born.

48

The Neolithic Era

The fundamental change in the eating habits of the first farmers had a great effect on their society. For the first time in the many thousands of years that man had lived on earth he was no longer a wandering hunter-gatherer.

The fields of grain needed to be tended through the year. In the spring these seeds had to be planted, during the summer the fields had to be kept free of weeds and birds and in the early autumn the crop had to be harvested. Even during the winter the people could not leave the land, for they had to protect

The earliest farming communities grew wheat and barley and kept flocks of sheep and goats.

the vast stores of grain from rats and mice. This meant that people were living in permanent villages instead of seasonal hunting camps. This new society marks what is called the Neolithic Era or the New Stone Age.

49

Because man was now settled down he could own much more than previously. When man lived as a nomadic hunter-gatherer he could own only what he could carry. But as a farmer, man had a permanent home in which to store his possessions.

He began to make new things which he could not have carried around with him. Perhaps the most important of these new inventions was pottery. This provided man with bowls to eat from, but, more importantly, pots in which to store food for the winter.

Within a few thousand years of the origin of agriculture, man in the Middle East was living a settled life. But it was not only in the Middle East that farming began.

Seven thousand years ago, agriculture began in Central America. But the early Americans did not grow wheat or barley, nor did they herd sheep and goats. They planted sweet corn and potatoes and kept the llama for meat and wool. In Eastern Asia people were cultivating rice and yams.

The widespread appeal of agriculture is simple to explain. Ten square miles of land were needed to support one hunter-gatherer after the Ice Age. But the same ten square miles could feed about one hundred and fifty people if they were farmers.

The advantages of farming led to it gradually being taken up in many parts of the world. By five thousand years ago, agriculture had reached Britain and was being practised all over Europe.

During the thousands of years which it took farming to spread, many new methods and techniques were adopted.

In Greece eight thousand years ago cattle were domesticated for the first time. Pigs were first farmed in the forest lands of Europe at about the same time.

By five thousand years ago, the wheat and barley had also changed. They were no longer the long straggly plants of the Middle East. Centuries of cultivation had produced a plant which gave more grain than before. The new types of wheat and barley were also able to grow in colder and wetter climates than their wild counterparts, making them ideal for cultivation in Northern Europe.

But perhaps the most important new invention in farming was that of the plough. For many years the ancient farmers had known that grain grew best on land which had recently been dug over, so they used digging sticks and hoes to dig over the soil. However, this took a long time and was very hard work for the farmer.

The invention of the ox-drawn plough about five thousand years ago changed the situation dramatically. It made the actual work of digging the land much easier for the farmer. This allowed him to cultivate more land, producing extra food or, if he wished, to spend more time on other activities.

It can be seen that by the time agriculture reached Britain it was already at a very advanced stage of development.

It was these Neolithic farmers of Britain and north-western Europe who were responsible for the most dramatic and mysterious relics of prehistoric men, the great standing stones.

The invention of the plough made man more efficient at growing crops.

The Megalithic Builders

Once farming communities were established in Europe, they began to erect monuments which can still be seen today. Some of these monuments are called megalithic. This is a Greek word that describes the giant stones used in their construction (*megas*, great and *lithos*, stone).

In Britain some of the earliest megalithic monuments are long barrows. Up to one hundred metres long, these mounds of great stones covered in earth were used for burials. The same people that buried their dead in long barrows also built henge monuments. A henge is a circular bank with a ditch inside it, both interrupted by one or two entrances. Sometimes the bank and ditch enclosed a circle of wooden posts

or standing stones (as shown above).

Some very impressive megalithic building can be seen around the village of Avebury in Wiltshire. Unfortunately, the great henge with its stone circles at Avebury has suffered much from decay and vandalism during four and a half thousand years since it was built. However, when it was first built it must have been one of the marvels of the age.

The great ditch and bank which surround the stone circles were hacked from the ground by gangs of Neolithic men using the simplest tools. Pickaxes made of deer antlers were used to loosen the natural chalk. The rubble would then probably have been scraped with shoulder-blade shovels into baskets, then dumped to make the bank. When it was completed, the steep-sided ditch – the continuous hole from which the

chalk had been taken – was all of nine metres deep and the bank towered six metres above this. Both the ditch and the bank would originally have been even more imposing than they are today just because Avebury stands on chalk. Consequently the green turf of Avebury would have been enclosed by two giant white rings.

Around the inner side of the ditch, a circle of standing stones some four hundred metres in diameter was erected. In all there were about one hundred stones in the circle, some of which weighed sixty tonnes. Within this outer circle were set up two smaller circles, one in the northern half of the henge and one in the southern half. An avenue of about two hundred stones ran for two kilometres over the hills to a smaller stone circle. It is possible that

Four thousand years ago the neolithic farmers of north-west Europe built many megalithic monuments, such as at Avebury.

another avenue ran in the opposite direction.

The stones used in the circles and avenues are sarsen sandstone boulders, which can still be found on the hills about a mile east of the henge. The transportation and erection of the stones must have proved a formidable feat for Neolithic man and his simple tools.

The architects of Avebury would first have chosen a boulder approximately the size and shape required. This would then have been dragged on rollers by hundreds of men to the henge. Once the stone was at the site, a pit would have been dug and, still with the use of rollers, the stone would have been dragged up to the edge of the pit. Then, using an ingenious system of wooden levers and props, the gangs of builders would have slowly raised the stone upright, so that its base rested in the pit.

Not far from the great henge at Avebury is the West Kennet long barrow with a megalithic chamber and also the unique and curious monument called Silbury Hill. This is the largest prehistoric mound in Europe and it was built about four thousand six hundred years ago. It is probably slightly older than Avebury itself. This artificial hill towers forty-three metres above the valley and its base covers well over two hectares. No burial has ever been found at Silbury and the purpose of this strange mound still remains a secret of the past.

About four thousand seven hundred years ago, a site forty-five kilometres to the south of Avebury was chosen for the construction of a henge bank and ditch. This site, now known as Stonehenge, must have been very important to many people because building was to go on there for the next thousand years. During this time, boulders of a special kind of stone, called bluestones, were brought all the way from Wales to build a stone circle. This was later changed to make way for the great sarsen circle. This final building phase was completed about three thousand six hundred years ago by people who knew about using metal to make tools. By this time, long barrows had gone out of fashion and people were buried under round mounds with pots, bronze tools and elaborate necklaces.

Although Stonehenge is smaller in area and contains fewer stones than Avebury, it is justly famous for its superior building techniques. The builders were no longer satisfied with erecting boulders of approximately the correct size and shape.

The stones at Stonehenge were very carefully shaped before they were set up.

Perhaps the most impressive of the architectural wonders at Stonehenge are the lintels. These are the stones which span the gaps between the uprights. Not only did the ancient builders have to raise them several metres off the ground in order to place them in position, but they were shaped so as to give a smooth curve to the outer edge of the monument. Furthermore, each lintel had a mortice hole in its underside which exactly matched a tenon on the top of the upright on which it rested. This jointing made the whole structure much stronger and more secure. The people who built Stonehenge were clearly master stonemasons.

The significance of the megalithic monuments such as Avebury and Stonehenge is very great. The number of men involved in the building work must have been phenomenal. Some of the stones at Stonehenge must have needed hundreds of men to move and erect them. When monuments such as Stonehenge were being built, Britain was inhabited by farmers living in small villages. It would appear that there must have been some form of central authority capable of organising people from many villages to build the great henges.

Some of the stone circles, Stonehenge in particular, are aligned with astronomical sightings. For instance, the midsummer sun rises over the heelstone at Stonehenge. Perhaps this indicates that the henges were temples to a sun god or places where festivals were held at certain times of the year.

The great monument of Stonehenge as it appeared after its final rebuilding in about 1600 B.C., when it was probably an important ceremonial centre. Overleaf, inter-tribal warfare became more common during the Bronze Age. Our illustration shows warriors of south-eastern Europe attacking a village.

54

The Coming of Metal

The people who built the sarsen circle at Stonehenge had an advantage over the earlier farmers in Britain. They knew how to work bronze. Before the invention of bronze, all the tools used by farmers and craftsmen were made of stone, bone or wood. These tools were quite efficient and continued to be used alongside a whole new range of bronze implements. However, stone weapons were not very effective and superior bronze daggers, spearheads and, later, swords and helmets were quickly adopted. Eyebrow tweezers, razors and horse ornaments were also made in bronze. Gold was used for many decorative purposes.

The major advantage of bronze over stone was that it could be cast. A skilled metalsmith was able to produce a tool of almost any shape, size and complexity. This property of bronze was put to good use by the prehistoric men to Europe, who produced a wide range of axes, knives and other tools.

By the time of the Bronze Age in Europe the human population had been growing steadily for centuries and may have reached a crisis point. All the best farmland had been occupied, so the extra people were forced to farm the less productive lands. Human nature being the way it is, it is more than likely that villagers began to argue with each other about who owned which piece of land and which village had the right to graze its cattle in a particular area.

The constant feuding between villages and tribes in Europe may have led to the rise of warrior chieftains. It was the duty of these leaders to protect their villages from attack and to lead assaults on other villages. The fighting men of the Bronze Age must have made imposing figures in their bronze armour and armed with the terrible new bronze weapons. Many of the Bronze Age burial mounds contain the remains of these men, who were buried with all their finery.

In the Middle East the increase in population and prosperity led to the founding of the first cities. It was in these cities that the urban society was born.

In an urban society people are generally richer than in a rural society. It is also possible for there to be a greater number of specialists, that is people who are very proficient at one occupation, potters for example. But the main feature of an urban society is co-operation. The people of a city will join together to build strong walls to protect the city or to construct irrigation channels to keep the fields well watered.

This urban society, which was emerging in the earliest cities, is the basis of our present-day civilisation.

About five thousand years ago, in the Babylonian city of Sumer, workers at the temple invented writing. Though it was probably invented to keep a record of land ownership or of tax payments, writing was soon being used to record important events. Some of these records have survived. We know the names of the kings of ancient Sumer, their actions and their behaviour.

Though it took many years for the use of writing to spread, and indeed many primitive societies do not use writing even today, the invention of writing marks the beginning of historic times and the end of prehistory.

The first cities, surrounded by strong walls, were built in the Middle East about eight thousand years ago.

Glossary

Acheulean – An early toolmaking culture.

Aegyptopithecus zeuxis – An ancestral pongid which lived some twenty-eight million years ago.

Aurochs – Extinct species of wild cattle.

Australopithecus africanus – A hominid which lived in Africa two million years ago, possibly one of man's ancestors.

Avebury – Centre of megalithic building in Wiltshire.

Bronze Age – The period in man's prehistory when Bronze was the main metal in use.

Cave Bear (Ursus spelaeus) – An extinct species of large bear.

Cro-Magnon Man – The earliest group of modern man to inhabit Europe.

Hominid – The name given to man and his ancestors.

Homo erectus – The earliest generally accepted human, which lived between one million and two hundred thousand years ago.

Homo habilis – Considered by some to be the first human, it lived one-and-a-half million years ago in Africa.

Homo sapiens – Our own species of man, which is divided into several subspecies.

Magdalenian – A toolmaking culture dating from fifteen thousand years ago, characterised by its use of bone and wood tools.

Megalithic – Term used to describe the large stone monuments of prehistoric Europe.

Mesolithic – The Middle Stone Age, the period in man's prehistory just before the invention of farming.

Middens – Large heaps of refuse left by Mesolithic fisher folk.

Mousterian – A culture of stone toolmaking associated with Neanderthal man.

Natufians – The first agricultural people, named after the modern village of Natuf.

Neanderthal man (Homo sapiens neanderthalensis) – An extinct subspecies of Homo sapiens.

Neolithic – The New Stone Age, the earliest farming society, before the invention of metal working.

Oldowan – The earliest culture of stone toolmaking, associated with *Homo habilis*.

Palaeolithic – The Old Stone Age, the period of man the hunter.

Paranthropus – A large, robust hominid, now extinct.

Plesiadapis gidleyi – An early primate from North America.

Pongid – The term used to describe the apes and their ancestors.

Prosimiae – A primitive group of primates, of which *Plesiadapis* was an early member.

Ramapithecus punjabicus – A seed-eater hominid from ten million years ago.

Steinheim man (Home sapiens steinheimensis) – An early subspecies of *Homo sapiens*.

Stonehenge – The most famous of all megalithic monuments.

Sumer – An important city of the ancient Middle East, where writing was invented about five thousand years ago.

Tundra – The environment prevalent during the Ice Ages, characterised by cold, treeless plains.

Woolly Mammoth (Mammuthus primigenius) – An extinct species of elephant adapted to the cold climate of the Ice Ages.

Woolly Rhinoceros (Coelodonta antiquitatis) – An extinct species of rhinoceros adapted to the cold climate of the Ice Ages.

Pronunciations

Aegyptopithecus zeuxis – ee-JIP-to-PITH-ee-kus zeus-ees

Australopithecus africanus – OSS-tra-low-PITH-ee-kus AFF-ree-carn-us

Coelodonta antiquitatis – SEEL-oh-DON-ta anti-quee-TART-iss

Homo habilis – HO-mo HA-bee-lis

Homo erectus – HO-mo ee-RECK-tus

Home sapiens sapiens – HO-mo SAY-peep-ens SAY-pee-ens

Homo sapiens steinheimensis – HO-mo SAY-pee-ens STINE-hime-EN-sees

Homo sapiens neanderthalensis – HO-mo SAY-pee-ens nee-AN-der-taal-en-sees

Mammuthus primigenius – mamma-THUS pry-mee-GEE-nee-us

Paranthropus – PA-ran-THROW-pus

Plesiadapis gidleyi – plees-ee-ah-DAP-is GID-lay-ee

Ramapithecus punjabicus – raamaa-PITH-ee-kus pun-jar-BYE-kus